chewed

Arne Svenson + Ron Warren

for Charles
and
for Joshua

Generally, by the time you are Real, most of your hair has been loved off, and your eyes drop out and you get loose in the joints and very shabby. But these things don't matter at all, because once you are Real you can't be ugly, except to people who don't understand."

Margery Williams Bianco
The Velveteen Rabbit

FOREWORD

Any dog or cat owner will speak of a favored toy that, in the course of being gnawed, shredded, punctured, torn, eviscerated, has become an indispensable companion to their pet. They will recount with wonder their pet's specific manner of ravaging this toy, or even try to convince you that a deliberate pattern of transformation is at work. But do they ever really *see* this bedraggled object of their beloved pet's desire?

This question arose when we visited a friend and were met at the door by her dog, who presented us with a slobbery mass of yarn and stuffing: the gutted remains of a handmade sock monkey. Having spent years photographing sock monkeys for a previous book, we were well aware of their "un-chewed" form. Intrigued that such a benign plaything had so readily become an eyeless, armless, one-legged monster, we realized that we had found our next project—portraits of chewed toys as seen through the eyes of the adoring chewer.

We began by coaxing these victims of tough love from pet-owning friends, some of whom confessed that they just *might* have an old pet toy or two lying around—only to produce an astonishing array of mangled remains. Soon we were inundated with boxes containing plush animals, rubber squeakies, and unidentifiable bits and pieces. During our photo shoots a number of owners insisted on waiting in the studio, refusing to budge until photography of "their" toy was complete, as if their housebound pet's sanity were on the line. Especially poignant was the delivery of cherished toys that had been held onto long beyond the lifetime of the pet.

Among the perpetrators responsible for the sorry condition of our subjects is a dachshund who rips the squeak boxes from plush animals' throats; pit bull Daisy who finds nothing more satisfying than delicately gnawing a rubber doughnut; and an Abyssinian who sends canvas creatures to heaven on catnip-scented clouds of fiberfill.

As our project evolved, it seemed that everyone had a favorite story relating to their pet and a toy. This led us to invite authors to contribute tales inspired by their favorite *Chewed* photograph. The results range from Roz Chast's humorous chronicle of the meteoric rise and precipitous fall of Gertie Lou, a "gorgeous duck" from Albany, to Andrew Zimmern's "Cautionary Tale," complete with a recipe for fried squirrel.

Our eyes have been opened. Now when a slobbery mass of yarn and stuffing comes our way, we recognize what the true gift is—the chance to witness the bond between a love thing and its maker.

Arne Svenson
Ron Warren

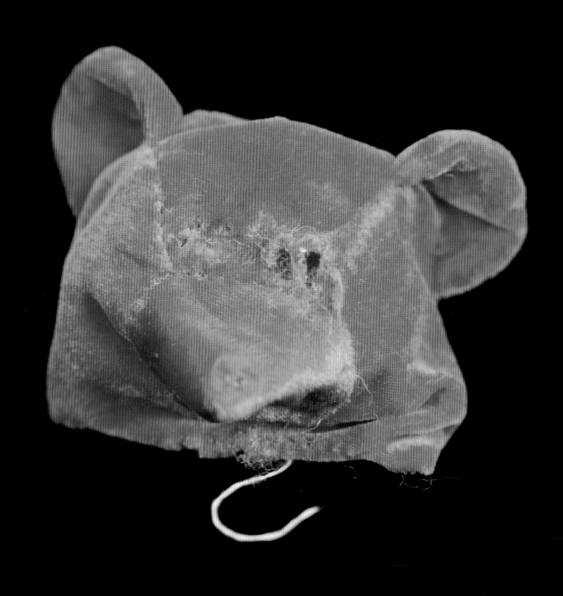

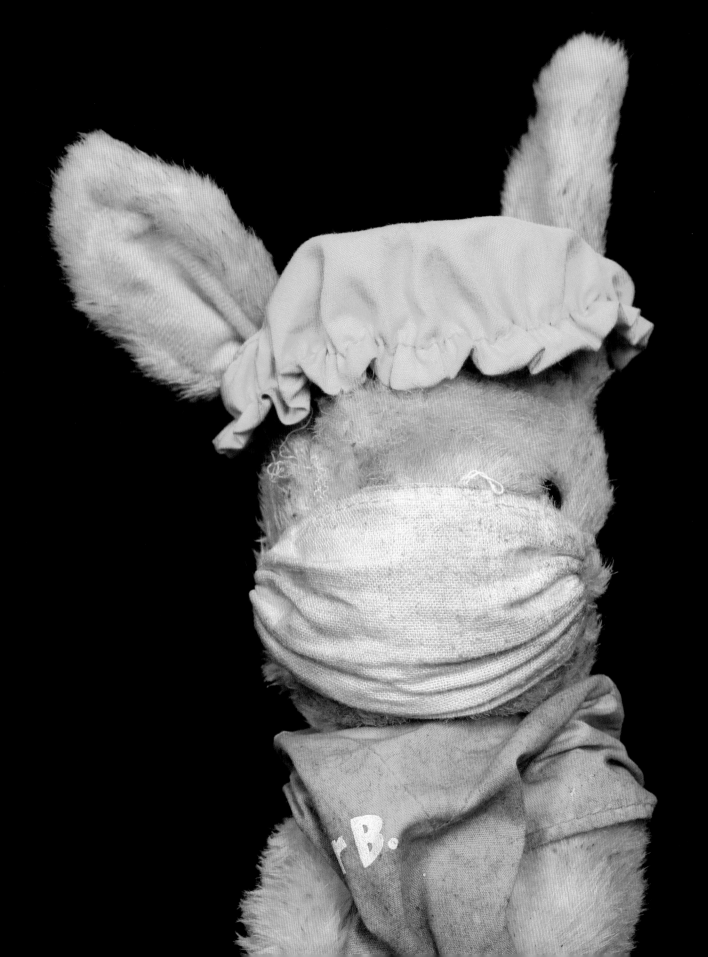

IT'S FRANK SINATRA'S WORLD (WE JUST LIVE IN IT!)

Nobody was a bigger Frank Sinatra fan than me! His phrasing! Those Ring-A-Ding charts Nelson and Gordon and Billy May laid down for him. I'd sit in the bin at the cheap Eat 'N' Go in Erie, PA, and do my Frank impression for my friends (A 99-cent pair of flip-flops and a bottle of Maalox!). I'd curl my lip and cup an imaginary cigarette like the Chairman did...the way Bogie taught him...like a sailor up on deck in a storm.

It was 1977. I knew Sinatra was appearing in town because the news rack was right in front of me. That's how I found out Elvis died "straining at stool," but that's a story for another day.

You get pretty jaded looking at the world from a plastic bin in an all-night mart. You see it all: minor stick-ups, kids trying to snow the owner with fake IDs, unwed mothers in dirty sweat pants sticking boxes of Froot Loops in the bubble jackets.... But you don't expect Frank Sinatra to walk in, his bodyguard Jilly Rizzo by his side—a man with a neck thick enough to plug the Grand Coulee Dam. At first I thought it was just a guy who looked like him, but those blue eyes! The good Lord only handed out one pair of those! Anyway, Frank came in for a copy of *Variety* and a bottle of Jack Daniels. Sinatra responded to the owner's apologetic "Sorry, Mr. Sinatra, we don't carry *Variety* and all we sell is beer" with a curt "Listen, Sabu! If I ever come back in here and you don't have a bottle of Jack I'm going to shoot your elephant." At that moment the most gorgeous woman I had ever seen—I'm talking legs up to here—walks in.

"Hey, Frank, I'm tired of sitting in the limo, how long are you going to be?!"

"Sorry, baby!" Frank said. "Here, doll, how 'bout a stuffed animal?" He told Jilly to grab me out of the bin, I couldn't believe it. Inside of three minutes I'd be in Frank's limo on my way to the Oliver Hazard Perry Music Hall to hear my idol sing. Frank handed me to the woman, laid a C-note on the counter, and left, the woman and Jilly right behind. I'd never been in a limo before—I don't know what Liberace's bathroom looked like but this had it beat by a mile!

Truth is?...I never made it to Frank's concert. On the way there the beautiful woman got mad at Frank for calling her Ava! Frank had half a bottle of Jack Daniels already in the car and was pretty lit, and all of a sudden he yanked me out of the girl's arms and started chewing on me and crying! The man who had made America swoon for close to half a century was tearing my fabric with his teeth, calling me "Ava," and begging me to drop the bullfighter and come back to him!

"Frank! Frank! That's not Ava! That's a cheap kid's toy!" Jilly yelled. I was too in shock to be hurt by Jilly's condescending attitude. Finally the big bull of a man ripped me from Frank's arms and tossed me out of the speeding car and I was hit and dragged thirty miles by a Wonder Bread truck.

I still love Frank's music but I no longer respect the man. Never meet your heroes!

TOM LEOPOLD

INTERVIEW

Q. Gracie.* What happened?

A. I can't remember the details. I blanked out. But I'll be honest I loved every minute of it. We'd been polite for years and then one day Georgie* just lost it and he started going for it.

Q. Is there any part of it you regret?

A. In my line of work it's what you expect. You come off the assembly line fresh and fluffy and you pray for this to happen. I don't know how I can explain it to you except to say it's what I'm created for.

Q. But from the looks of things there was violence.

A. Violence? Are you kidding? Try *Ecstasy*!

Q. Did you learn anything?

A. I learned to surrender. To live my life. I faced my worst fears and was delighted with the outcome. Okay, maybe I'm not as beautiful as I was ten years ago but who is? I considered plastic surgery but I hate it. It's so obvious and desperate. Better to look your age.

Q. What's the bow about?

A. Are you kidding? It's my identity. Frilly? Yes. And maybe to some a bit saccharine. But I'd be nothing without this bow. I might as well just chuck it if that were the case. Optimism runs my life. Perverse optimism. Also I think it's only polite to try and look your best.

*names changed to protect privacy.

ISAAC MIZRAHI

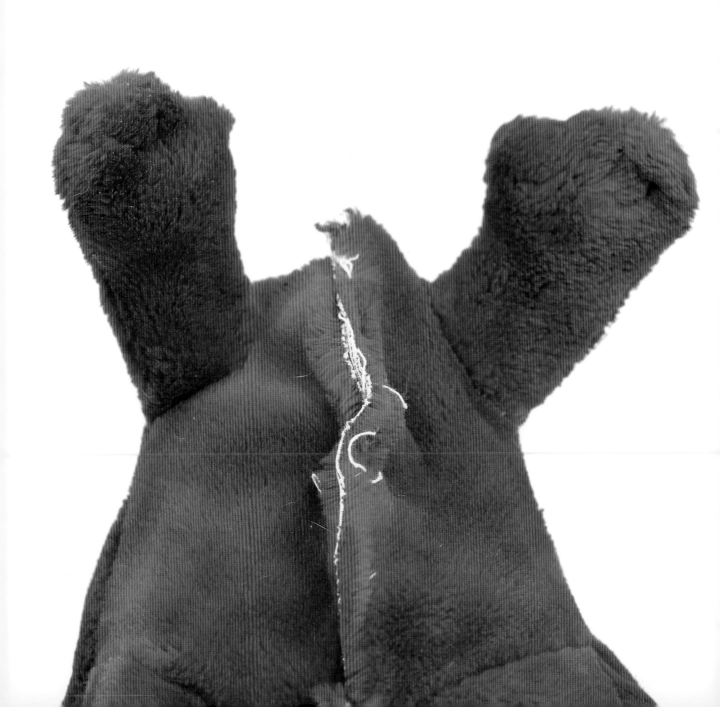

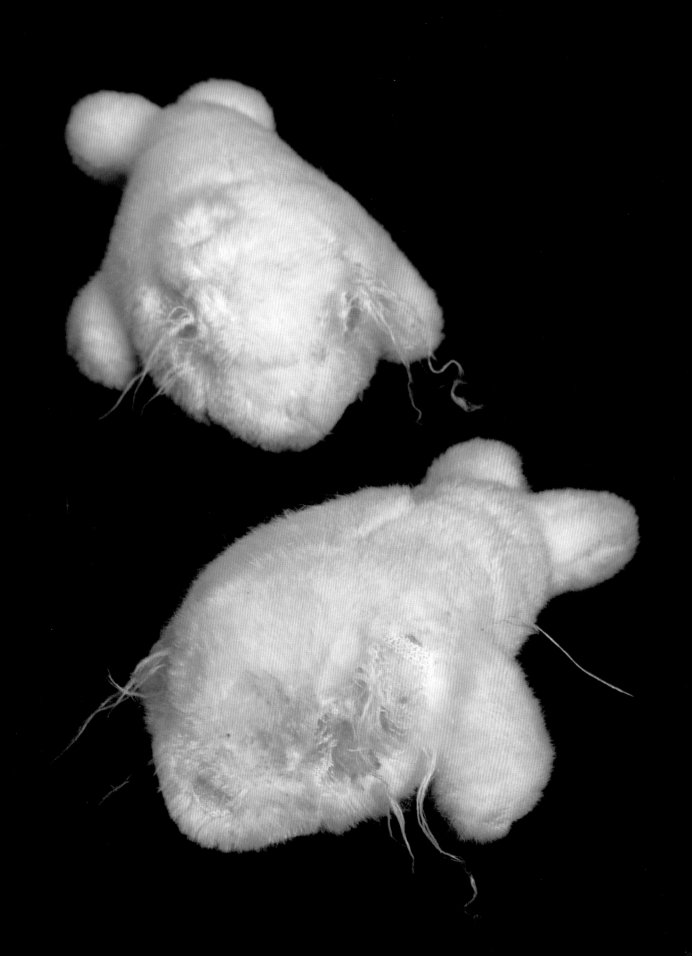

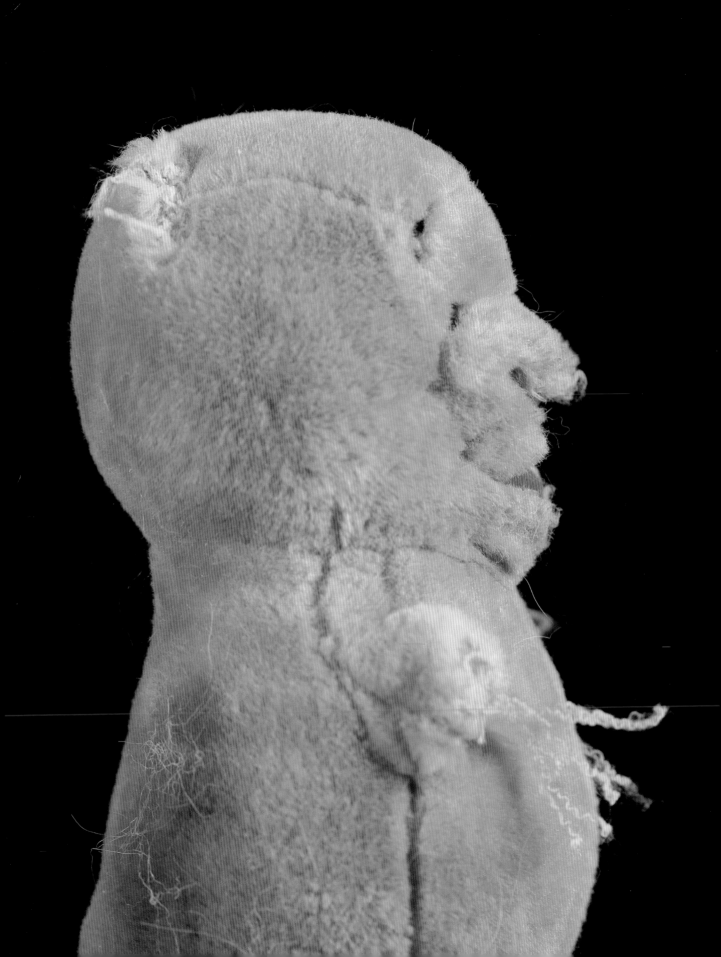

GERTIE LOU

I used to be a gorgeous duck. I lived on a quiet, nice pond in back of a condo outside of Albany, New York. I had glossy feathers and a long neck, just like a swan, I swear to God. You never saw a neck like that on a duck. Never. Shiny black eyes. A bill other ducks would kill for. A perfect bosom. I had the whole package.

One day, I'm swimming around, playing with a paper cup, and suddenly this seagull I never saw before is swimming around in front of me. He's a kind of runty guy with thin, patchy feathers and nicotine-stained bill, and he's wearing sunglasses and a like Hugo Boss jacket. I try to avoid him because he's giving me the creeps. But I don't like being rude. It's not how I was brought up. So anyway, he paddles up beside me.

All my instincts are saying, "Get away, Gertie Lou! Paddle away NOW!" But he was a real sharp character, that one. Right away, he's saying things like, "What are you, a model?; where's my marshmallows, I could toast one on you, you're so hot." Stuff like that. He told me he was an agent and that he would take me to New York and make me a big star. As you can see, I was a very naïve duck back then. So I leave my friends and family without even saying good-bye. Next thing I know, we're flying into Kennedy. And within a month, I'm "Gala, America's Favorite Duck." Yeah, that was me! I know! Hard to believe, looking at me now.

Anyway, like I said, it didn't take long before I had it all. A sensational career, a giant loft in Tribeca, money to burn, famous friends.... For a while, I was on top of the world. But easy come, easy go.

Long story short: I started hanging around with a pretty fast crowd and got into Colombian finely ground corn. I was putting about a thousand bucks worth of the stuff up my nose a day. As you can see, I only have one nostril now. I lost all my feathers, and they never grew back right. One night at a club, I lost both eyes. I was so high I didn't even know it until the next morning. And worst of all, I wrecked my beautiful, beautiful neck. I had to have this operation—never mind. What's the difference? I lost it all.

But I don't want to be a total downer. I'm just saying: if you see a seagull in sunglasses, don't feel bad about giving him the cold shoulder. Just swim away.

ROZ CHAST

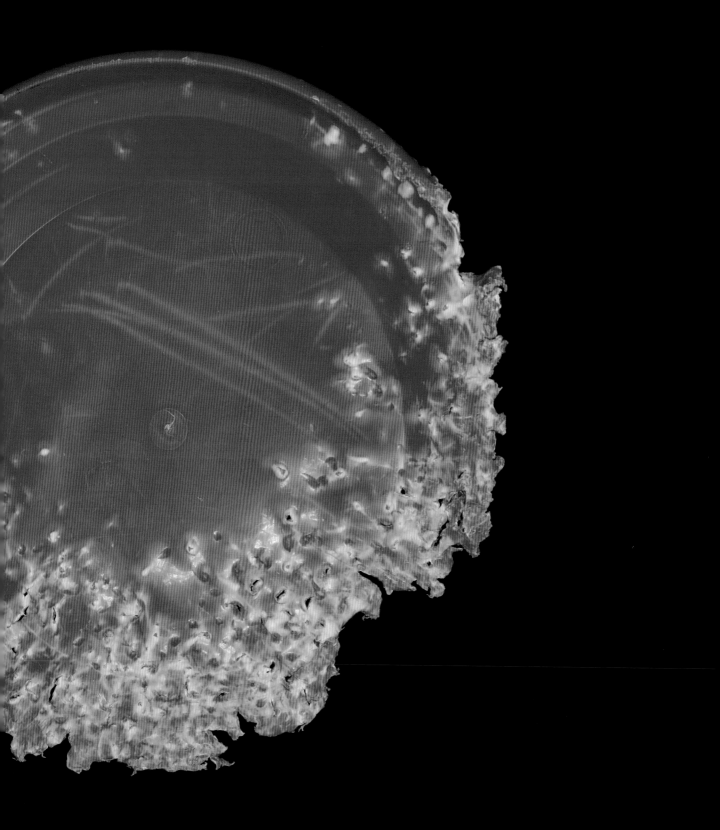

BUSY ANN

I thought I was shopping for a sweater but I ended up meeting the love of my life. When I first saw her being dangled in the air in the hands of a shopkeeper she clearly had under her spell, I couldn't have known about the eye thing. But I sure found out that night.

The shopkeeper empathically shared that this beauty's name was Ann (no *e*, she's too busy for an extra letter) and that she was born in February, which explains the perfect brown heart-shaped spot on her side. Ann is a smart and elegant sophisticate with remarkable calm and composure, but all of that flies out the window when she gets a new toy. She has amassed well over a hundred of them at this point, and she still has her first one, Taz. She takes great care of her toys as soon as she finishes chewing their eyes out. When I found Taz newly blinded, his big plastic eyes near his feet, I thought it happened because she was teething. But then it happened again. Up next was a Beanie Baby gecko that never saw it coming. It only takes her about 3 minutes to gouge a pair of eyes out, and apparently it must be done at once. Ann is a wildly social little creature except for those special 3 minutes when the world disappears as she frantically chomps on retinas. Once the maiming is complete, they are hers for life.

I have wondered if Ann's need to maim precisely is because she doesn't like being stared at or because she has a great disdain for plastic. I kind of understand on both counts, but she has removed cloth eyes and a plastic nose or two, so I am not exactly sure. On occasion a whole face needed to be removed, as evidenced by one of her all-time favorites, a red-and-yellow bear that now has exposed brain matter and a single black thread dangling from its mouth. But the very second her eye teeth alterations cease, she takes great care of them and causes no more harm. I have yet to figure out how that black thread became attached at the mouth; it wasn't there when I gave it to her.

If Ann were asked to choose her all-time favorites, I think she would pick the Beanie Babies. I know they were not meant as dog toys, but I figured if children could chew on them, they would be fine for her. Plus, it is really fun to see a dog round the corner with a hippo hanging out of its mouth. Ann keeps them in a big pile that looks either like a lot of fun or the scene of a horrific massacre, depending on your point of view. I recall the complete disgust and horror on the faces of the Beanie Baby vendors as I tore off their sacred heart-shaped labels rendering them uncollectable by all but dear Ann.

TODD OLDHAM

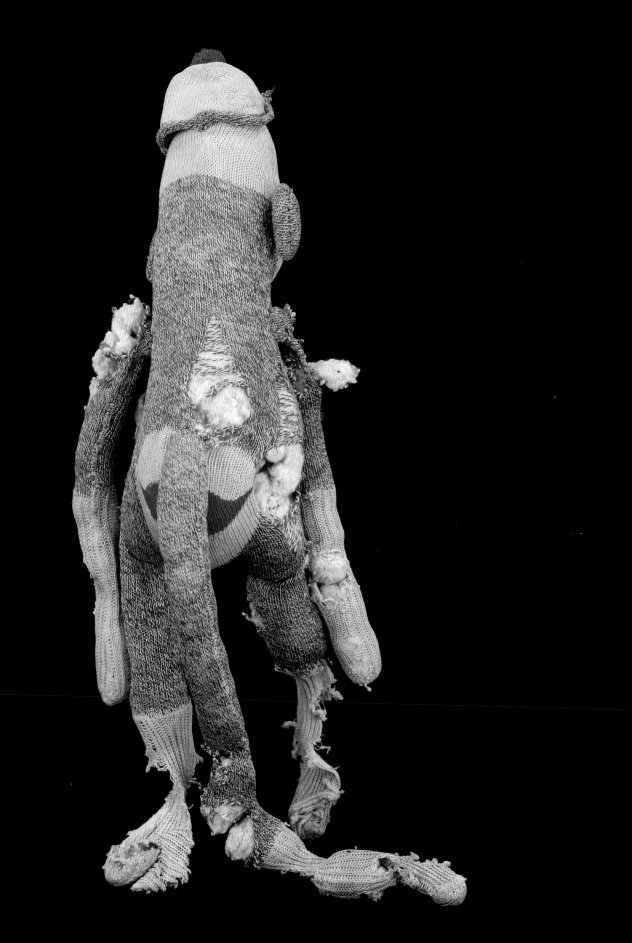

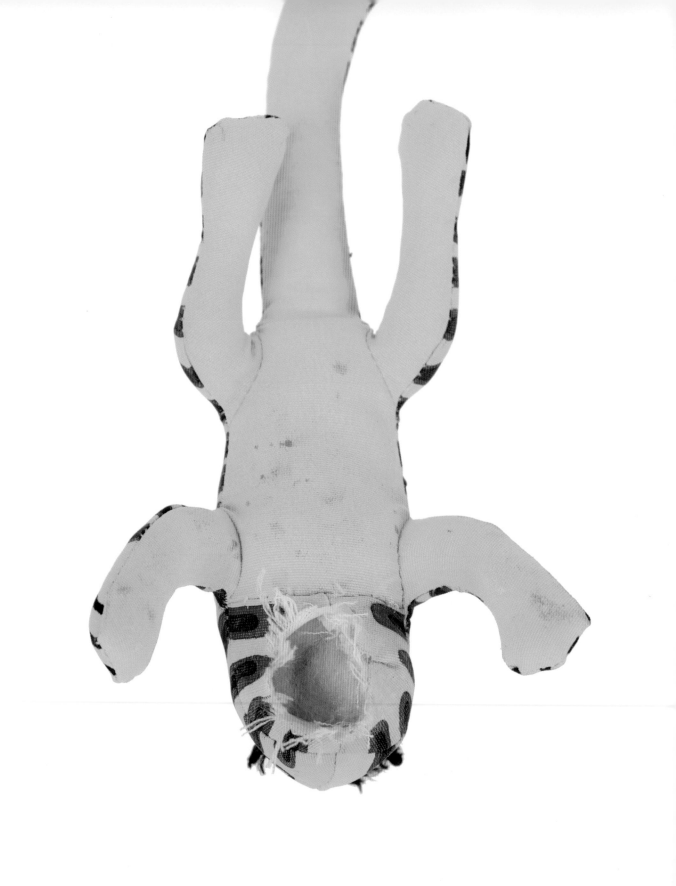

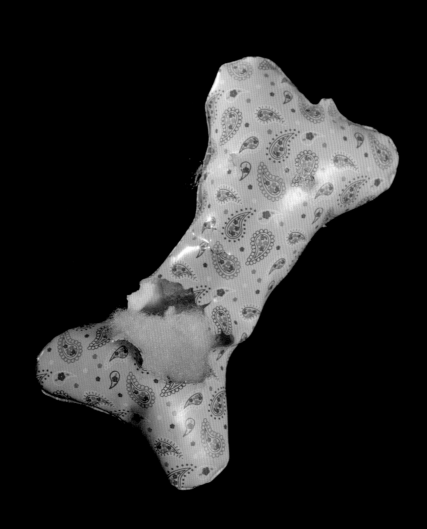

WITH THESE HANDS

Though Bunny is now missing the upper half of its body, one can easily imagine the lack of hesitation Dog displayed as it plucked Bunny's black button eyes from its face, the satisfying snap of thread as the flat discs popped from the soft skull.

The entire head was obviously devoured. And no matter how cute those floppy, bent-at-the-tip ears may have been, they were not cute enough to stop Dog from seizing and pulverizing them with his wolf-powered, drooling, gaping maw.

Bunny's throat was gleefully sawed open with inch-long front incisors, esophagus stuffing flying through the room as Dog shook his head violently, rabidly from side to side.

Torso? Gone. Belly? Gone.

In a bold, taboo-defying moment of canine insanity, Dog consumed Bunny's left arm. This act clearly provided no satisfaction or joy, for the right arm remains unscathed, as if in apology.

Because in the ten thousand years dogs and people have lived together, dogs formed a special reverence for *hands*. Hands toss treats made of meat into the air for catching. They lay buttered spaghetti noodles over the nose, which is both confusing and thrilling, and they scratch exactly right behind the ears.

Only the daintiest, most tentative nibbles were taken from Bunny's carrot-soled feet (which Dog knew weren't even real feet at all). Of course *feet*, to a dog, are merely less coordinated and mildly retarded *hands*.

Dog knows Bunny is not a real rabbit. Dog also knows he can do anything he wants to Bunny and not get into trouble. It's okay to hump it or cuddle up with it and then eat its eyes.

But because of Bunny's somewhat anthropomorphized features, it is to Dog less a symbolic rabbit and more a symbolic person in a rabbit costume. To Dog, Bunny is a small trick-or-treater. Or a furry.

And it is this humanity, no matter how cartoonish, which has spared what remains: those parts of a person a dog loves most.

AUGUSTEN BURROUGHS

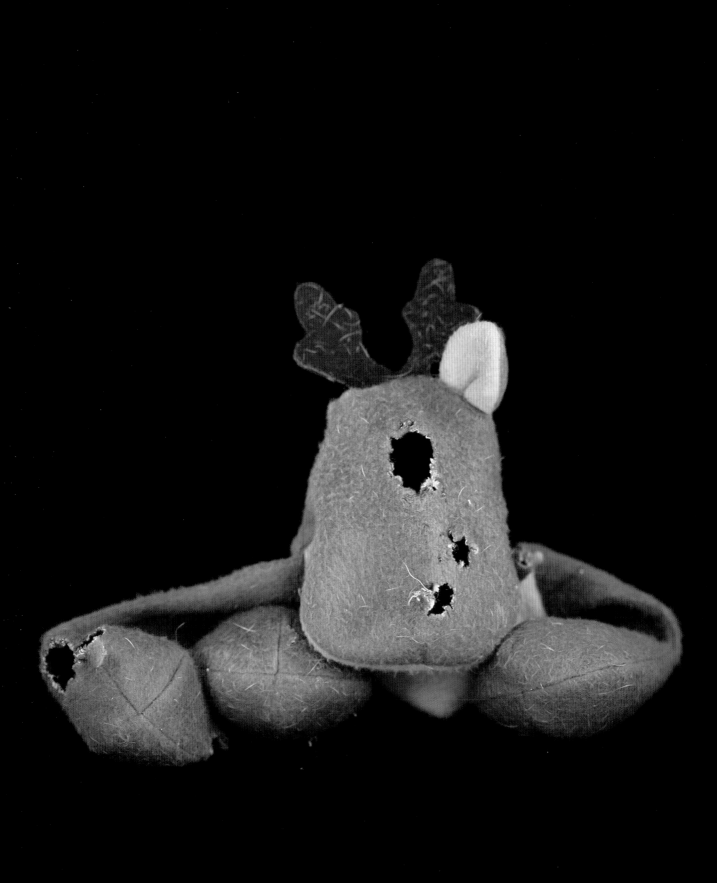

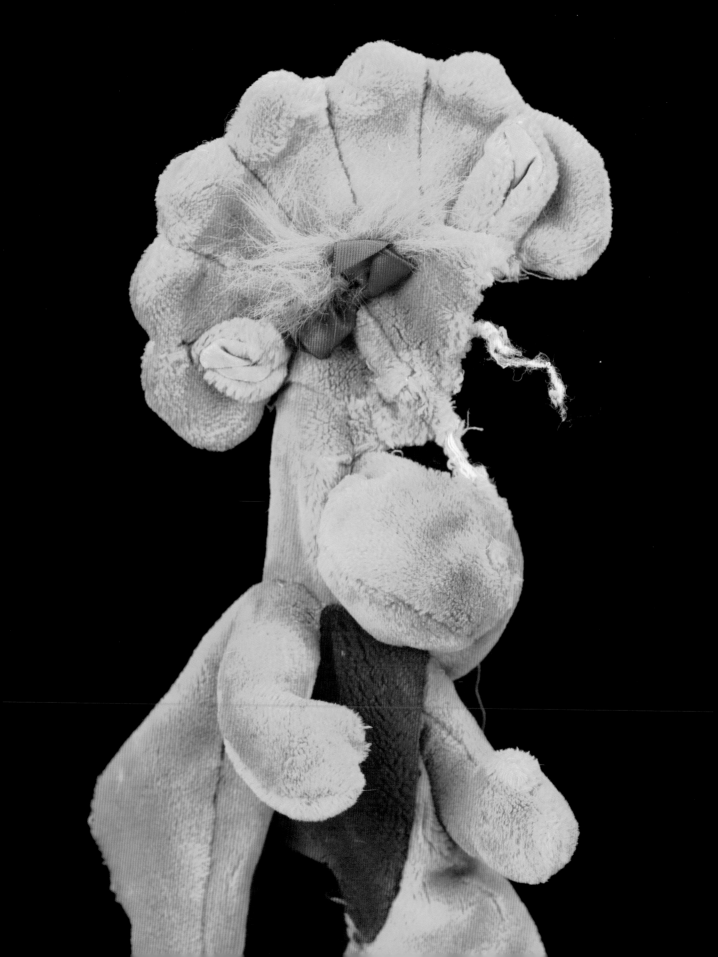

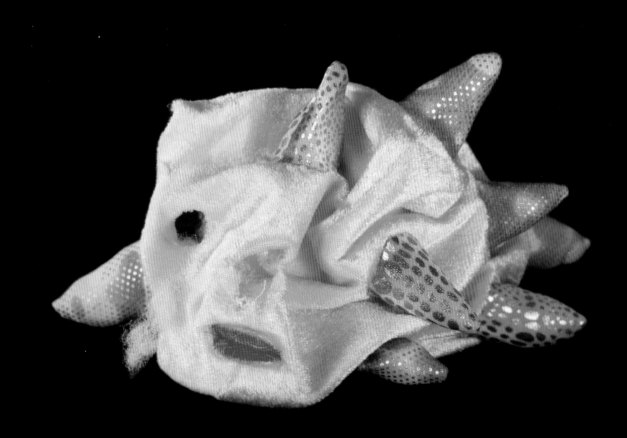

SQUIRREL: A CAUTIONARY TALE

I knew I wanted to eat it. Why wouldn't I? I had joyfully devoured this primeval delicacy years before, in the hollers of West Virginia and yeah, it was really fucking good. Never shy away from a plump squirrel, that's my motto.

I know what you're thinking. And to answer your question, this squirrel has nothing in common with a NYC Central Park squirrel. Those little bastards are vicious and Lord only knows what they are eating or what squirrel-borne pathogens they could pass my way. This squirrel was different. This squirrel was local...born, raised, fed, and eventually taking the long dirt nap, all in the backyard of my house in Minnesota. He ate apples I tossed him in the winter, berries from my garden in summer. Diet dictates flavor!

One day in late October, small-game license in hand, when preparation met with opportunity, I culled the herd and dispatched the biggest, fattest, sweetest, fruit-and-nut-fed squirrel of all. This was locavorism of the highest order. Zero-mile dieting more or less. I skinned and butchered him, roasted the head in the fireplace, engaging the most far-reaching places of my lizardy consciousness as I cracked the skull and prized out the brain, splashed it with sea salt and a squeeze of lemon and savored every blissfully creamy, meat-buttery moment. The rest of him? Well, fried squirrel is something my friends at the Snowshoe Lodge gave me a lust for, so lunch was a no-brainer. Pun intended. Weeks later a treat arrived in the mail from the local taxidermist, so up on the shelf went my little squirrel. In full view through the glass-enclosed porch of all the other critters in the woods. Top of the food chain, baby! But my delightfully articulated symbolic gesture was short-lived. The pooch, drawn to the latest incarnation as much as I was to the first, somehow got him down. And yes, the dog clearly enjoyed his chew toy as much as I enjoyed his warm-blooded doppelgänger.

Fried Squirrel   *serves 1*
1. Take your squirrel and skin it, clean it, rinse it in several changes of cold water, and pat dry. Cut it into fifths (two front quarters, two rear quarters, and one central piece of the saddle).
2. Let it soak in a cup or more of buttermilk for as little as 2 hours or as many as 24.
3. Remove the squirrel from the buttermilk and let it drip dry for a moment, then coat well with sea salt and freshly ground black pepper. Dredge it in flour lightly seasoned with salt and pepper and set pieces aside on a sheet of waxed paper.
4. Place a large cast-iron skillet over medium heat and add rendered fresh lard (vegetable oil will do in a pinch), to fill skillet about a half inch. Heat the fat to 375°, or until a piece of squirrel sizzles well when slipped into the pan.
5. Fry pieces for 5–6 minutes, until walnut brown, drain on paper towel, season, allow fried squirrel to cool a few minutes, and enjoy.

ANDREW ZIMMERN

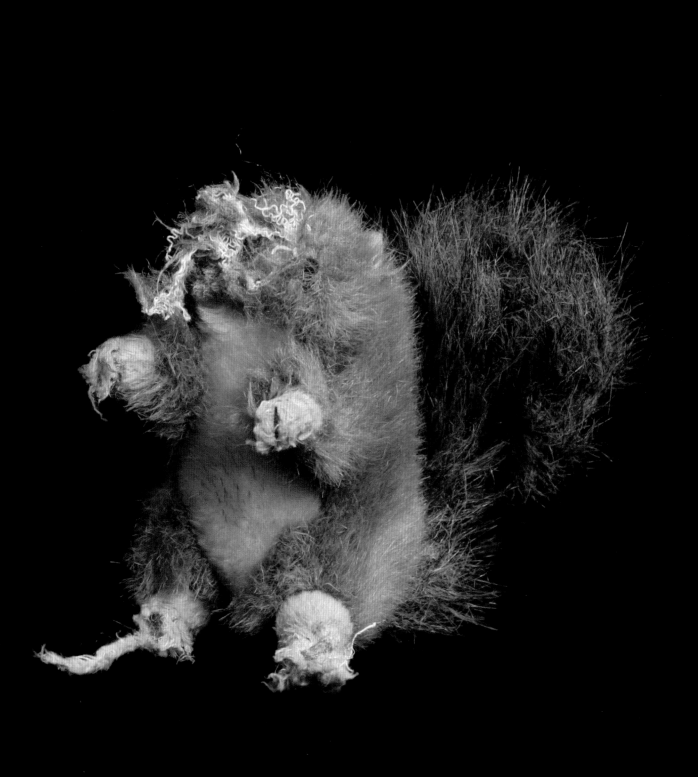

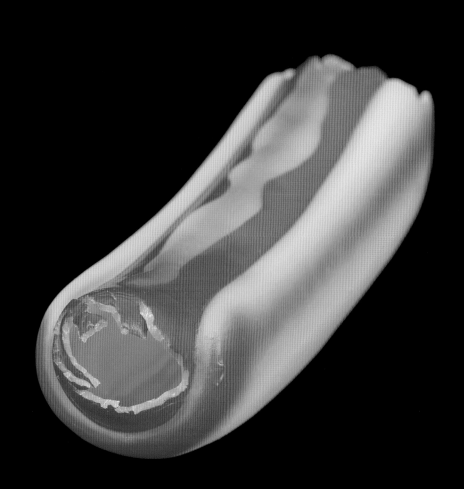

CHEWED CLASSIFIEDS

Chance Meeting!

Saw you at the dog park last Friday dangling from mouth of a border collie. I thought we had something. Email me! Weirdwally@hotmail.com.

LOST: Right leg, foot.

Boston terrier ran off with the damn thing. If found, please return to: Fuzzy the Bunny, c/o The Walker Family, 312 Burnham Lane, Modesto, CA.

Discarded? Left out with the trash?

Ignored by children and family pets? Maybe it's your fault. Stuffed toy/ plushy encounter group meets every Thursday at 7 PM behind the Wassersteins' garage on Corwin Street. Ask for Blinky.

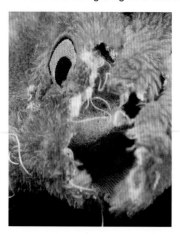

Dr. Mitzler's Stuffed Animal Outpatient Clinic.

Fur grafted, eyes burnished, paws reattached, antlers replaced, unsightly teeth marks lasered. Affordable rates, free estimates. 1-555-865-3321.

Stuffed rhinoceros seeks new situation.

New owner tied a pink ribbon around my neck and named me "Margueritte." Frankly, I've never been so humiliated. Contact Mar...oh, crap, I mean, Buster! 555-654-9962.

Flopsy: I don't care

if you're covered in dog saliva; I love you. —Mister Butterscotch

Stuffed toys needed for transporting goods

across U.S. border. Contents will be sewn inside you, removed on arrival. Please have updated passport. Unique opportunity! Paolo, PO Box 9, Juarez, Mexico.

Stuffed-toy self-defense classes starting now.

Tried of being torn to pieces by bratty toddlers and vicious pets? Former Navy Seal will teach you the ancient art of Muay Thai. Call Master Kwan, 1-800-CHEW THIS.

FRANK SANTOPADRE

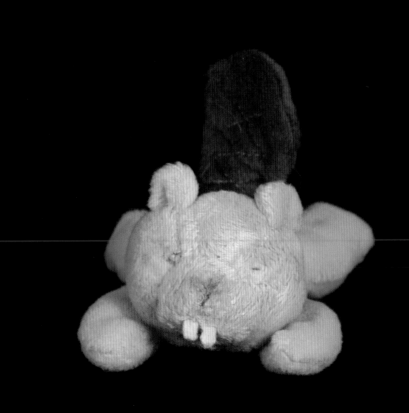

THIS BEAR

This bear once belonged to my first dog, Man Ray. My second dog, Fay Ray, was also acquainted with this bear. I found it in my cabin in Maine almost thirty years after Man Ray last had it with him in 1981. Ray was very attached to this bear. I was forever taping and sewing it up. Once on a trip across country I left it in a motel in Montana. So distraught was Man Ray that I had to drive back to get it, more than 200 miles.

    When not in Maine we lived on the top floor of a tall building in New York City. This bear fell out of the open window and Ray jumped out after it. Thank god this didn't happen.

WILLIAM WEGMAN

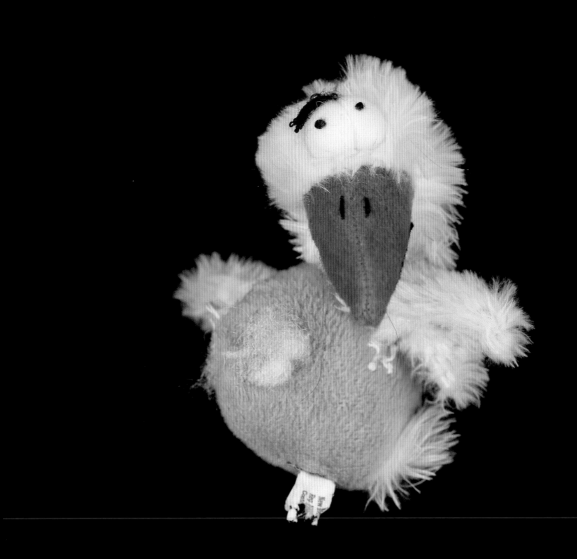

LOVE LETTER FROM A DOG

the dog ate the shoe.
the dog was alone
and a little bored
and a little sad
and longing for his person.
his friend. his mate.
and what was the closest thing to the person.
the shoe.
the scented sweet little shoe.
in new york city alone, each day, ten thousand shoes are chewed up.
all over the country, all over the world.
millions of shoes are being devoured.
longing. loneliness. chewing. missing.
and what is the finale.
yelling.
but really.
it is a love letter after all.

MAIRA KALMAN

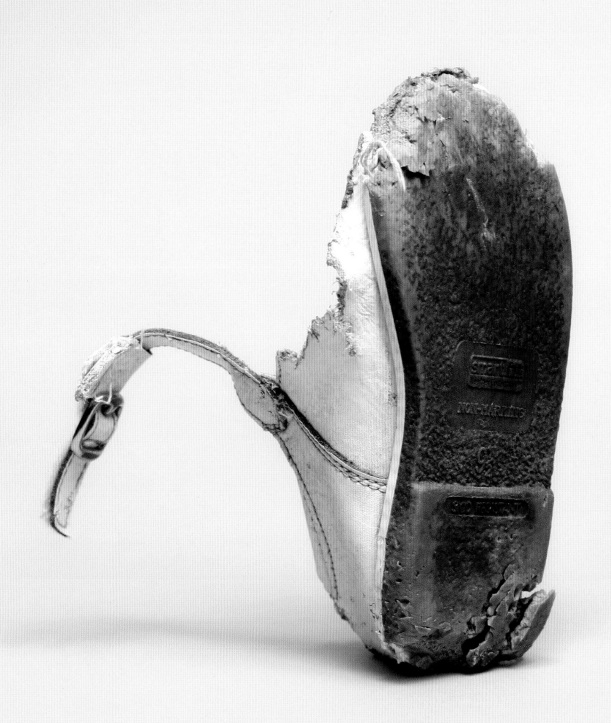

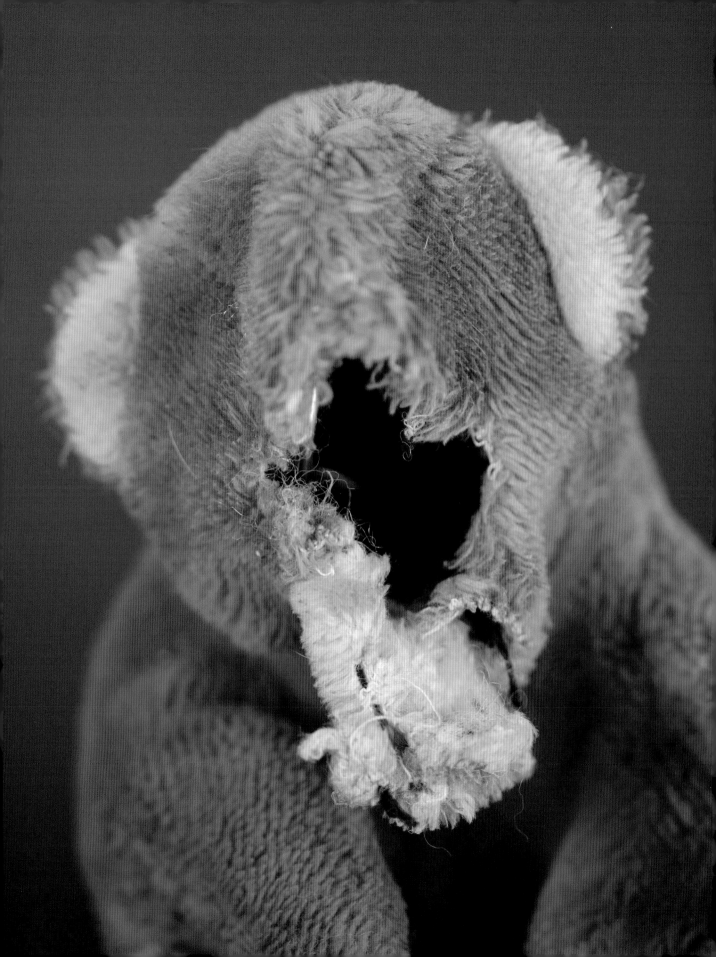

WOLF MIND, DOG HEART

When the terrier got old, it was soft toys she wanted. Thick blue pull-ropes sat in corners and tennis balls bounced idly by my feet. I bought Bunny for my nephew, with fur velvety as a kitten's coat and two glossy black eyes knotted beneath perfectly flopsy ears. As soon as I set him down, that orange-haired terrier's mischievous lips were around Bunny's ear and her spiky white teeth dug right through him. In a flash the terrier was pulsing her jaw like a drum at his neck. I'll admit to watching for a moment, transfixed by the rhythm, so by the time I'd pried him out, Bunny's damage was beyond cosmetic. I thought, doll hospital, yes, but stuffed animal infirmary? Was there such a place?

Luckily I knew a dentist who was deft with stitches—I'd gone earlier that year to have my gums sewn up, and the whole process was so famously painless that he'd tacked the postcard I'd written on his wall. Bunny and I hit the streets quick, mopy in the mouth but fast with purpose. The dentist's impression was printed firm on his face; Bunny's last days of lying in linen were dangerously near. I waited reading magazines until news came.

Back at home the terrier circled, sniffing. "Bunny's gone," I told her, fluttering my fingers. "No more." She stood stiff as a starched shirt, then lay down flat to the ground, her paws neat, crossed like bunched flowers.

SOPHIE ROSENBLUM

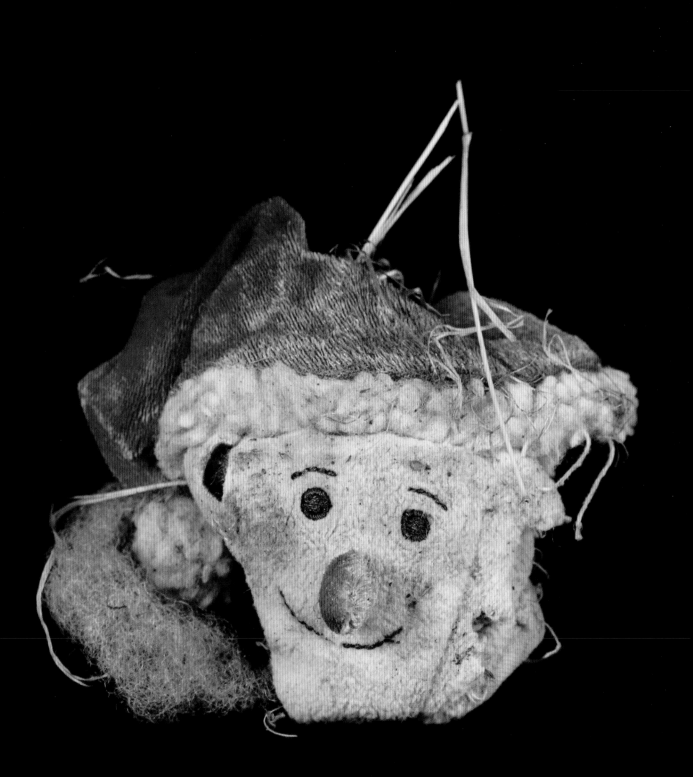

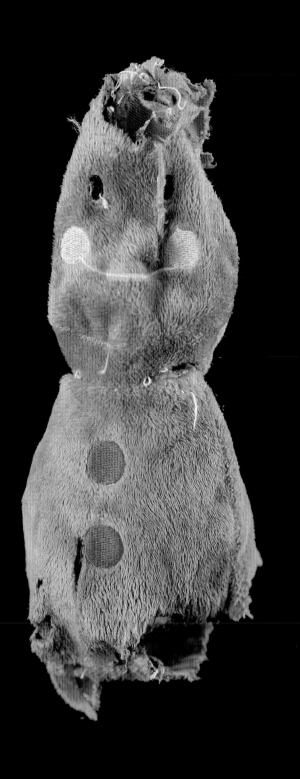

LOVE HURTS

Never get divorced in California. When they say you split everything down the middle, they mean *everything*. What hurt most is that I was there from the beginning — a corny Hollywood story you've heard a million times, but I really thought they were different. I'd been a prize in the free throw game at the Santa Monica pier for almost a year; it's not that nobody wanted me, they all did, but I was always just out of reach (10 in a row), til he came along, Johnny Nesbitt.

He was hoping to make it as a free agent with the Lakers — Lila was a Laker girl — but only til she got her break as a singer and they ran off to Vegas and got married. It was love at first sight, for them and for me: Lila just had to have me, and after 10 bucks' worth of tries, Johnny did it. Lila named me "Lucky," and our first night together was magic — a walk on the beach, dancing at one of the hot clubs, and she never let go of me until they got back to the apartment and made love. It was uncomfortable lying there next to them, but I got used to it, and soon couldn't live without it.

A few days later I lived up to my name when Lila got her big break. A TV producer, sitting courtside with Jack Nicholson, cast her in his new Reality show, *The Real Cheerleaders of the Pros*. On the third episode (the one where the referee exposed himself) she got to sing, and you know the rest from *People* magazine, *Entertainment Tonight*, and the tabloids: overnight stardom.

Johnny wasn't as lucky. He blew out his knee and his chance in the pros. His disappointment, the prescription drugs, and Lila's skyrocketing career were more than he could handle, and the fact that she took me everywhere didn't help. I think seeing us on *Letterman* during his third rehab pushed him over the edge. I was wearing a tuxedo and she sang her new hit "Lucky in Love" to me. Funny how the high point of one life can be the low of another.

Their relationship turned into a remake of *A Star Is Born*, as she kept getting bigger and Johnny became more of a drawback every day. He became abusive — not to her but to me. When Lila noticed the daily damage, he blamed the dog, and she eventually got rid of him instead of Johnny, but when I disappeared and the toilet backed up, she put two and two together and called a plumber and a divorce attorney. *Sixty Minutes* covered it as "Divorce Hollywood Style," and in his rage, Johnny broke into the house, ripped me in half, and left a note, "It's time for me to get a little Lucky."

We still don't know where Johnny and the bottom half of me are, but I hold no grudge and wish them only the best. I am writing this from our house in St. Tropez. — Luc

BILL PERSKY

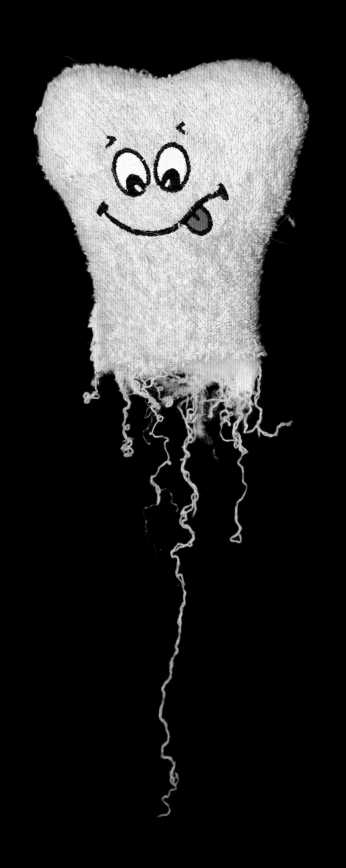

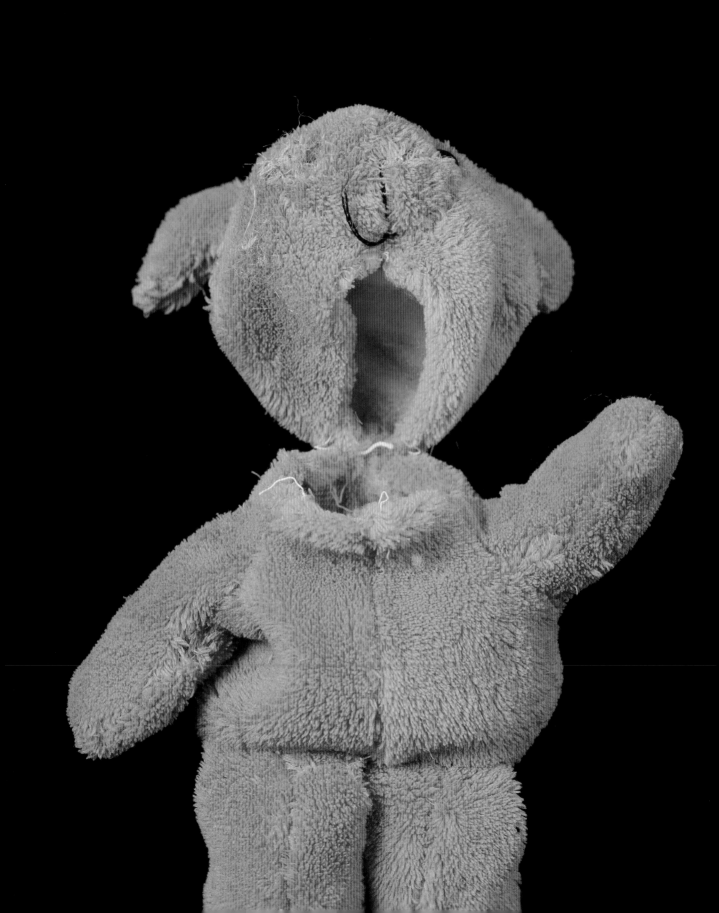

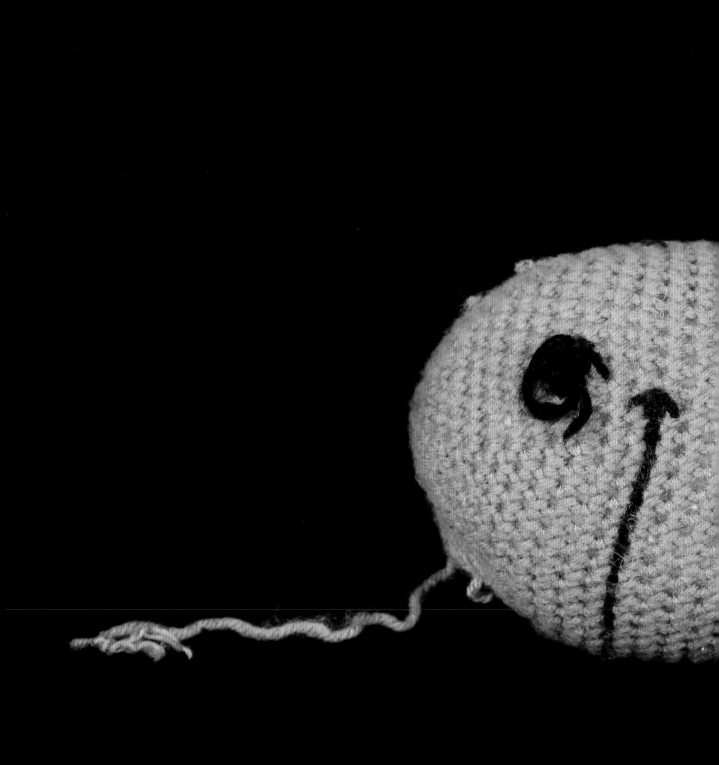

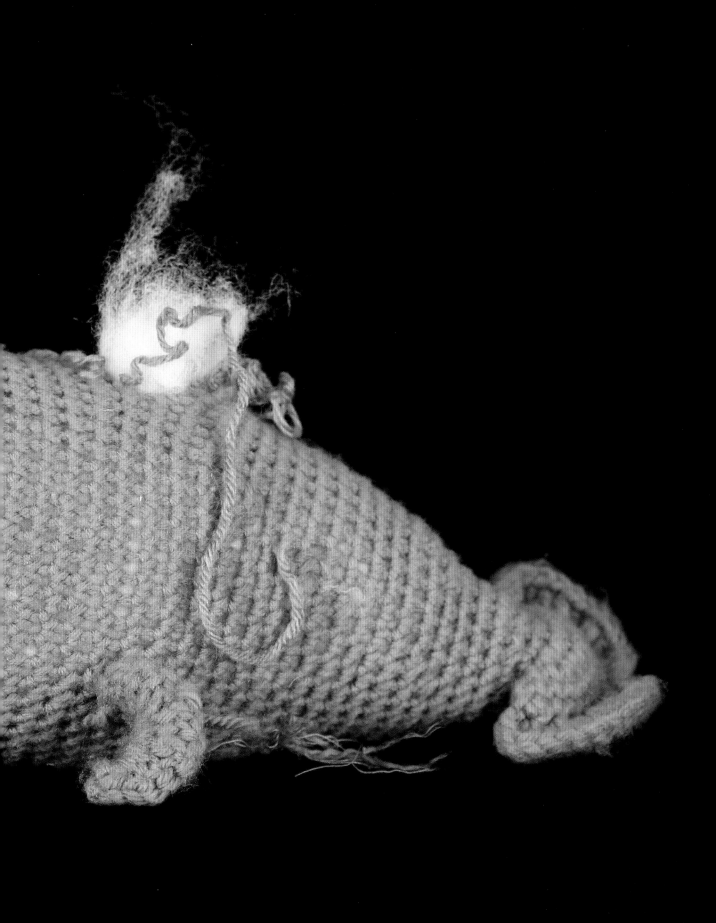

POLYPHEMUS

Let me tell you about Odysseus. He's not the nicest guy who ever strapped on sandals. He's duplicitous. Don't take my word for it, ask the Trojans! And he's murderous. Talk to Penelope's suitors—if you can find one he hasn't killed. He has this little boy thing that makes women go for him big time. You know: "I'm lost, and I'm far from home." Circe ate it up. What a gullible Siren she is! But look, I didn't say that. I don't want Circe getting angry at me. I have enough trouble without her turning me into a swine.

I think my life has been a lot more wholesome than that of Odysseus... Holy Uranus! Ever notice how much like "odious" that sounds? With me, what you see is what you get. I think of myself as a loving person, and I've got a huge playful side. Although maybe Galatea would tell you different. What can I say? We were kids. She gave me one smile, and I thought she loved me. All right, so I acted like a schmuck and crushed her boyfriend with a boulder. But that was six millennia ago, and she's still talking about it like it was yesterday!

I keep a low profile for a Cyclops. I cook. I drink a little wine. Only a little. You want to corroborate that, talk to my sheep. I don't think you'll find a single one that will have a divergent opinion—they are, after all, sheep. All right, I jest. But they are! They have their own Facebook page. Check it out.

My name, Polyphemus, means "famous everywhere." But Odysseus gets all the good press. His continuing fame just makes my blood boil! What's with James Joyce for instance? I loved *Dubliners* and *Portrait of the Artist*... But he lost me when he named his next book *Ulysses*. When I first heard about it—I was in Paris—I thought, "Oh, spare me!" I mean, would it have killed him to name the book Polyphemus? Hey Jim! Write a book about *me* strolling through Nighttown. Give me a wife named Molly! She won't cuckold *me*. I'll crush her with a boulder!

Perhaps I've said too much. Yeah, I know there are two sides to every argument. I'll even concede Odysseus may have a point. After all, I did eat most of his crew. They were *delicious*! Still, I think we can agree he overreacted when he blinded me with a wooden stake. Sure, I hold a grudge, but I'd be willing to have a drink with him and talk it over. Maybe we'll even shake hands and let bygones be bygones. Then I'll crush him with a boulder!

RICK MEYEROWITZ

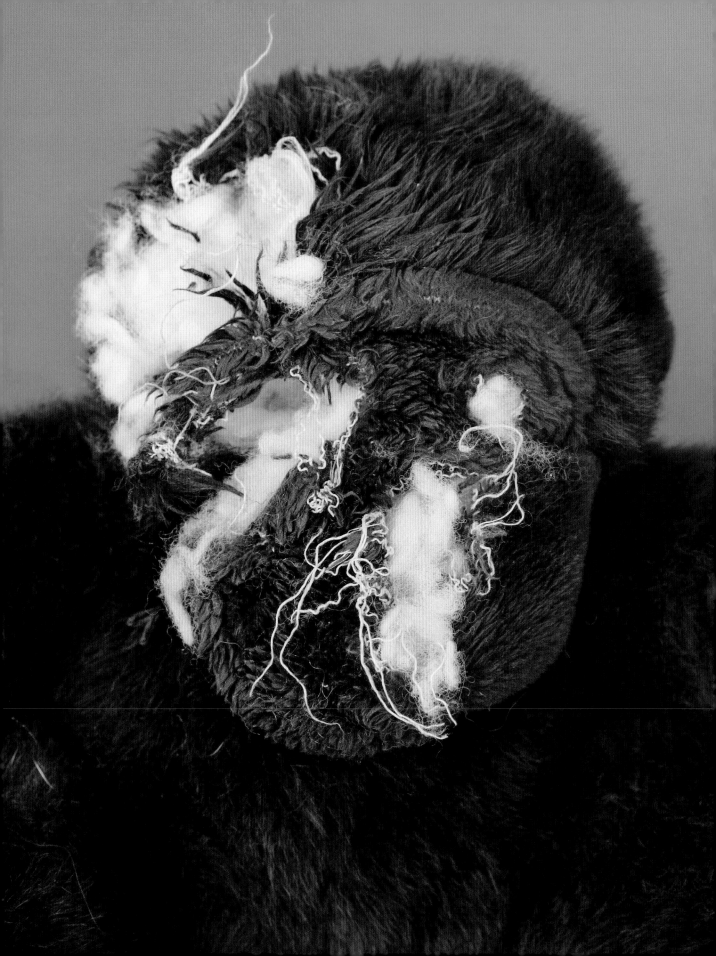

CRIME OF PASSION

Somebody loves me, is obsessed with me, crazy loves me. At first, he was only watching me, then stalking me, then smelling me. But he loves me so bad he blinded me, bit out my eyes, chewed off my nose, my ears. I can no longer smell. All he left me is my whiskers. All I hear is a constant rhythm pulsing as though I live underwater. I think about music and write my own lyrics, then rearrange them. I give my songs titles: "Sun Song," "Fish Song," "Happy Song," "Hunting Song," "Breakfast Song." I sing a rhyming song in my mind about high tides and the rotation of the moon. If I'm thirsty I imagine drinking water from a shiny, pink copper faucet or sipping from my private fountain where I scoop up lazy fish and eat them. I imagine a tureen of milk, a plate of liverwurst, and a wishing well. Everything I see is my creation. Everything I think is true. I am never alone; there are many delights. Somebody loves me.

DAISY FRIEDMAN

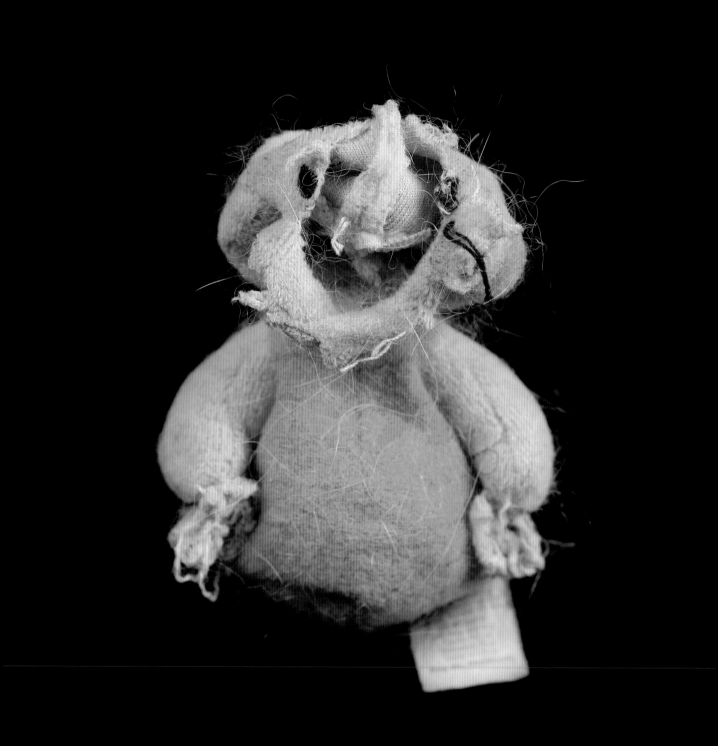

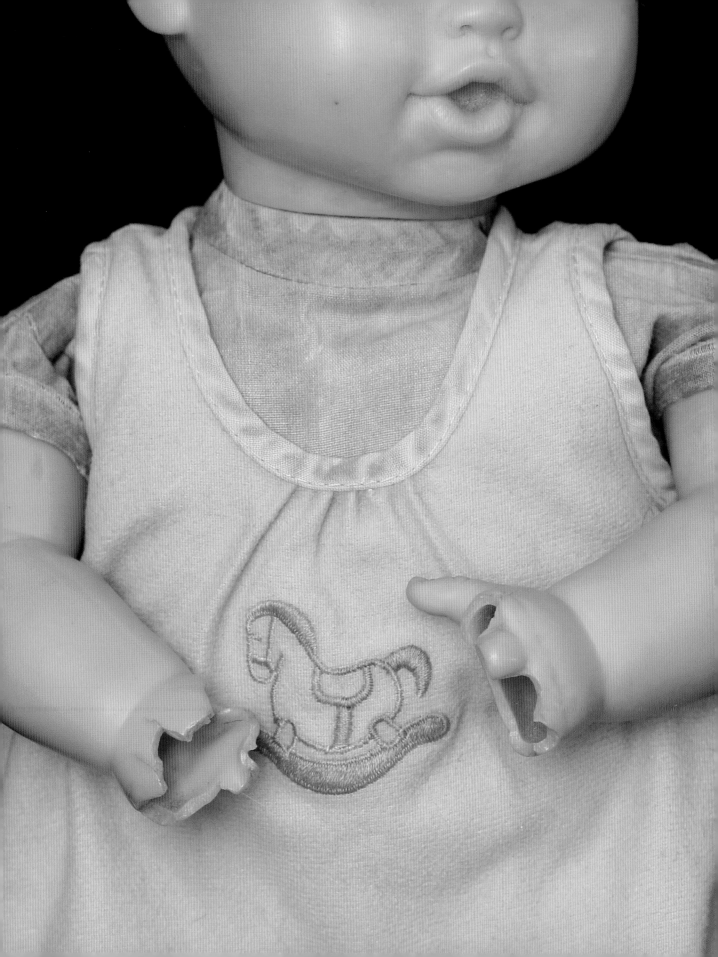

ACKNOWLEDGMENTS

Thanks to:

The Baumrin Family
Brice Brown and Donald Joint and **Daisy**
Monkey Burkhalter
Kris and Carrie Chatterson and **Tilda Bee**
Russell Crotty and Laura Gruenther and **Blaze**
Margot Gordon and **Baby Jane**
Tracy Granger
The Gruendemann Family
Ann Haskell and **Spunky**, **Yoyo**, and **Baby Sister**
Laura Lindgren
Marcia Lucas and **Baby** and **Bo**
Leigh Mozes and **Scout**
William Neil and **Wrigley**
Gloria Nusse and **Murdering Maggie** and **Lovely Lucy**
Todd Oldham and Tony Longoria and **Ann**
The Orr Family and **Sumo**
The Reed Family and **Bear**
Amy Rodriquez and **Alfredo**
Jane Rosenblum
Julie Saul and **Vicki**
Christopher Schelling and **Rio**
Dana Schmalenberg and **Bodhi**
Gabriel J. Shuldiner and **Mr. Wolfgang "Shibi-Shiro" von Cisco** and **punKpaws**
Kristina Svenson and **Taz**
Ken Swezey
Liza Todd Tivey and the late **Buster**
Belinda Todd and Scott Hanley and **Pluto**
Elizabeth Warren and **Barley Peanut Butter**
Martha Warren
Janet West

CONTRIBUTORS

AUGUSTEN BURROUGHS is the *New York Times* bestselling author of three memoirs, *A Wolf at the Table*, *Dry*, and *Running with Scissors*; three essay collections, *You Better Not Cry*, *Possible Side Effects*, and *Magical Thinking*; and the novel *Sellevision*. His work has been published in more than twenty-five countries. He lives in New York City with an Italian greyhound named Wiley.

ROZ CHAST has contributed over 1,000 cartoons to *The New Yorker*. Her cartoons have also been published in *Scientific American*, the *Harvard Business Review*, and *Travel & Leisure*, as well as many other magazines. Every so often she develops craft obsessions like decorating Pysanky eggs, origami, knitting, making tiny books, and fashioning clay miniatures of household appliances.

DAISY FRIEDMAN is a writer living in New York City.

MAIRA KALMAN is an author/illustrator who has lost twelve pairs of shoes for the love of a dog.

TOM LEOPOLD has written for television on such shows as *Seinfeld*, *Cheers*, and the BBC's *My Family*, on which he also served as executive producer. With Harry Shearer he wrote *J. Edgar!* *(A Musical Fantasia on the Life of J. Edgar Hoover)*. He is the author of three novels, *Almost Like Being Here*, *Somebody Sing*, and *Milt and Marty (The Longest Lasting and Least Successful Comedy Writing Duo in Show Biz History)*, and lives in New York City with his wife and their two daughters.

RICK MEYEROWITZ barks, pants, and begs for food in New York City. He is a prolific illustrator who recently published *Drunk Stoned Brilliant Dead: The Writers and Artists Who Made the National Lampoon Insanely Great*, a juicy bone of a book well worth chewing on.

ISAAC MIZRAHI is a leader in the design business for more than twenty years. He has been awarded four CFDA awards, including a special award in 1995 for the groundbreaking documentary *Unzipped*. Television audiences have come to love Isaac as the host of his own series on both the Oxygen Network and the Style Network and on Bravo's *The Fashion Show*. When not working, Isaac enjoys spending time with his dog Harry, cooking, and watching the Yankees.

TODD OLDHAM is an author, photographer, and designer who lives and works in New York City. He is currently working on his thirteenth book, a monograph on the artist Alexander Girard. As usual, he remains in constant adoration of his dog Ann.

BILL PERSKY is a five-time Emmy Award–winning writer, director, and producer for such shows as *The Dick Van Dyke Show*, *That Girl*, *Sid Caesar*, *Bill Cosby* and *Kate & Allie*. Of late he has compiled a memoir of stories, both professional and personal, which he performs as a one-man show, *Whisper Whoopie*. He is a contributing writer to *USA Today* and a guest lecturer at NYU and Yale University.

SOPHIE ROSENBLUM is a writer whose work can be found in journals, newspapers, and websites. She is at work on her first novel.

FRANK SANTOPADRE has created material for dozens of performers and personalities, including Bill Murray, Matt Lauer, Meryl Streep, Joy Behar, and Donald Trump. He has developed and polished stand-up acts for national headliners, and his work has been seen on ABC, HBO, Comedy Central, ESPN and TV Land, as well as in the pages of *National Lampoon*, *Vanity Fair*, and *The New Yorker*. He is also the author of *Pride and Prejudice* and the *Dead Sea Scrolls*.

WILLIAM WEGMAN lives in New York with his sixteen Weimaraners. He is married and has only two children.

ANDREW ZIMMERN is the James Beard Award–winning host, co-creator, and consulting producer of *Bizarre Foods with Andrew Zimmern*, author of *The Bizarre Truth*, and is a contributing editor and columnist with *Mpls. St. Paul Magazine* and *Delta Sky Magazine*. Follow him at andrewzimmern.com.

IDEAL
WORLD
BOOKS

ISBN 978-0-9722111-7-8

Designed by Laura Lindgren

Ideal World Books
Available through D.A.P./Distributed Art Publishers
155 Sixth Avenue, 2nd floor, New York, NY 10013
telephone (212) 627-1999
www.artbook.com

Printed in China
First Edition 2011

10 9 8 7 6 5 4 3 2

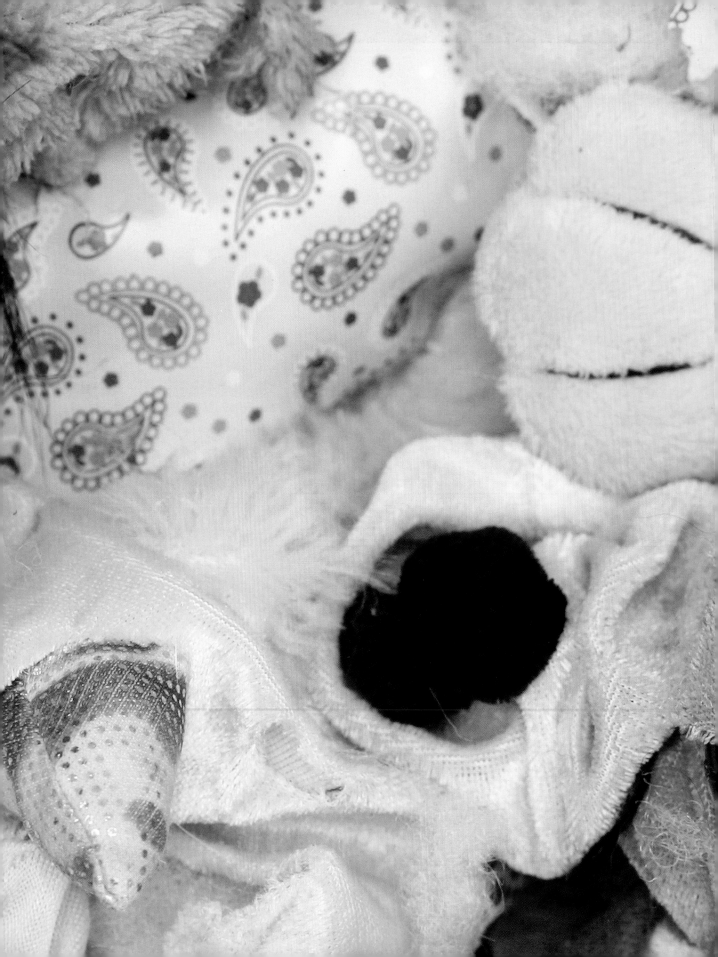